Native American Crafts

of California, the Great Basin, and the Southwest

By Judith Hoffman Corwin

Franklin Watts

A Division of Scholastic Inc.

New York Toronto London Auckland Sydney
Mexico City New Delhi Hong Kong
Danbury, Connecticut

For Jules Arthur and Oliver Jamie, and for the makers of these wondrous and beautiful things, who, through the ages, in many different ways, paint, sculpt, and sing of the Earth.

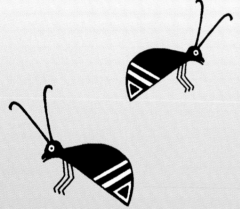

Book design by A. Natacha Pimentel C.

Library of Congress Cataloging-in-Publication Data
Corwin, Judith Hoffman.
    Native American crafts of California, the Great Basin, and the Southwest / by Judith Hoffman Corwin.
        p. cm.
        Includes index.
        Summary: Provides step-by-step instructions for craft projects based on traditional crafts of the Pomo, Zuni, Pueblo, Navajo, and other Native Americans of the Western and Southwestern United States.
        ISBN 0-531-12199-2 (lib. bdg.)   0-531-15592-7 (pbk.)
        1.Indian craft—Juvenile literature. 2. Indians of North America—Industries—California—Juvenile literature. 3. Indians of North America—Industries—Great Basin—Juvenile literature 4. Indians of North America—Industries—Southwest, New—Juvenile literature. [1. Indian craft. 2. Handicraft.] I. Title.
TT23.6.C67 1999
745.5'08997—dc21
                                       98-31449
                                          CIP
                                          AC

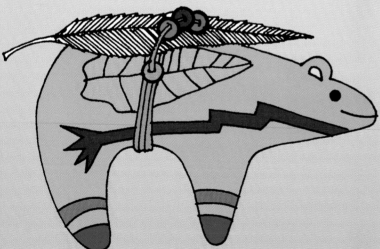

Published simultaneously in Canada
Printed in the United States of America
1 2 3 4 5 6 7 8 9 10 R 11 10 09 08 07 06 05 04 03 02

Contents

About the Native American Crafts Books

O our Mother the Earth,
O our Father the Sky,
We bring you the gifts that you love.
Then weave for us a garment of brightness;
May the warp be the white of morning.
May the weft be the red light of evening.
May the fringes be the falling rain.
May the border be the standing rainbow....

—Tewa Song, Southwestern Pueblo

Native Americans are believed to have been the first people to arrive on the North American continent thousands of years ago. They developed rich cultures based on their respect for the natural world around them—the Earth, sky, wind, rain, animals, plants, fire and water, the sun, the moon, and the stars.

The spirit of nature is important to Native Americans, and the design and decoration of the objects they use in their daily lives—to raise families,

to farm, to hunt, to defend themselves, or to make war—reflect the elements of nature. The designs on their clothing, pottery, baskets, dwellings, and weapons are decorative and are also an appeal to the goodwill of the spirits of the natural world. Native American people have no word for art because creating art is an integral part of life.

Now many Native Americans live in cities. Yet they often return to their home reservations to visit families and for special occasions. Their past is kept alive through storytelling and through arts and crafts. Traditional crafts, like the stories, are handed down from generation to generation, carrying along a cultural message.

The Native American Crafts series of books introduces young people to the cultures of Native Americans and to their creative work. We can learn about and appreciate Native American culture and incorporate what we learn into our lives through making art objects inspired by their examples. The projects in these books are based on crafts of everyday life, but do not involve ritual or religious objects. ◼

Native Americans of California, the Great Basin, and the Southwest

For thousands of years, Native Americans have lived in the beautiful, hot, dry lands of California, the Great Basin, and the Southwest.

California

In California, good soil and climate provided a plentiful supply of food. The Pomo people living in this area hunted deer, squirrels and other animals, and various birds, and collected plants and berries. Acorns were another important food source. They were ground into a fine powder that was used as flour. The Pomo have long been known for their fine, tightly woven baskets that they ornament with feathers and shells. They also use colored feathers to decorate dance costumes, hairpins, woven belts, necklaces, and headbands.

NORTH AMERICA

PACIFIC OCEAN

CALIFORNIA

GREAT BASIN

SOUTH WEST

GULF OF MEXICO

ATLANTIC OCEAN

N W E S

The Great Basin

The Great Basin is a large area between the Sierra Nevada Mountains in the west, and the Rocky Mountains in the east. It is centered in Nevada, Utah, Oregon, and Idaho. The traditional cultures of the Great Basin varied from desert dwellers and hunter-gatherers in the south and west, to horse-riding big-game hunters in the north and east. As nomadic people, the Great Basin Native Americans tended to have few possessions, and this is reflected in their arts and crafts. Great Basin tribes include the Ute, Paiute, Shoshoni, and Washo people.

The Southwest

The Southwest is an area of little rain and few rivers. It is rugged country of flat-topped mountains, called mesas, and steep-walled canyons. There are yellow-pine forests, and strings of purple-colored mountain ranges. The summers are dry with a burning hot sun and the winters are cold with strong winds and snowstorms. The Native Americans in this region speak different languages and form different groups, including the Pomo, Ute, Apache, Zuni,

Hopi, Navajo, Taos, Acoma, San Ildefonso, and Santo Domingo. Although some live in villages and towns, many work as farmers. They use irrigation techniques to bring water to their dry land and raise corn, beans, squash, and cotton. They also herd sheep and cattle.

These people are skilled potters, weavers, jewelers, and basketmakers. Some of their designs are centuries old, and their art often includes images connected with water—rain, clouds, lightning, fish, snakes, frogs, and "rainbirds." And in Pueblo villages along the Rio Grande River, the people still live much as their ancestors did. Ancient dwellings are still seen high up in the mountains. The world of the spirits and religion are important parts of the traditional way of life.

Here's What You Need:
- small wooden or straw basket
- colored permanent markers or acrylic paints and brushes, newspaper
- feathers or paper and pencil, scissors
- string or yarn, shells, beads, buttons

Here's How You Do It:
- Draw one of the simple band designs shown here on a basket, using permanent markers.
- Collect some bird or pigeon feathers and paint them with acrylic paints. (Acrylic paint can stain, so cover work surfaces with newspaper.) If you have no feathers, draw some on paper, color them with markers or paint, and cut them out.

10

Pomo Basket and Decorated Feathers

The Pomo people of California make beautiful baskets and decorate them with shells and with feathers from the woodpecker, bluebird, meadowlark, quail, and mallard duck. The Pomo give the baskets as gifts and use them for special occasions. We will decorate a ready-made basket and add strings of feathers, shells, and beads to make a special gift basket.

- Tie 6 inch (15 cm) lengths of string or yarn to the bottom end of each feather. Attach shells, beads, or buttons to the strings.
- You can also string several decorated feathers together to make a necklace, or start a collection of decorated feathers.

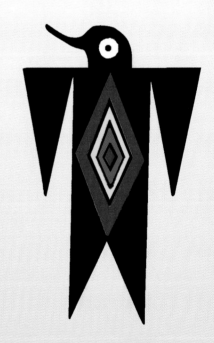

Here's What You Need:
- tracing paper, white oaktag, pencil
- colored markers, fine-line black marker
- felt, scissors, glue, tape

Here's How You Do It:
- Trace the outline of the horse and transfer it (page 46) to oaktag, or draw it freehand. Go over the lines with a black marker. Color it in with markers. Cut it out.
- Cut a scrap of felt to make a saddle blanket. With colored markers, draw patterns on the felt. Glue the blanket on the horse. Draw designs on the horse.
- To make a stand for the horse, cut a 2 inch (5 cm) by 5 inch (12.5 cm) strip of oaktag. Tape the short end to the back of the horse so it will lean on the stand.
- These handsome Ute designs can also be used on note cards or bookmarks

Ute Miniature Horse

The horse is important to the Ute people of the Great Basin. They make a variety of horse equipment—saddles, blankets, stirrups, ropes, and saddlebags. Distinctive designs, such as rows of geometric patterns, are painted on or formed with beads. We will make a miniature horse decorated with Ute designs.

13

Here's What You Need:
- homemade clay (page 47)
- paints, brushes
- permanent markers

Here's How You Do It:
- Take a tennis-ball-sized piece for each bowl. Shape the clay into a ball.
- Push your thumb down into the center of the ball. Gently push the clay out from the center to shape the bowl. The walls of the bowl should be about 1/4 inch (6.2 mm) thick.
- Bake the bowl (page 47) and let it cool.
- Paint the bowl white or a solid color and let it dry. If you can, paint the inside too.
- With a black marker, draw designs on the outside of the bowl. If the opening of the bowl is wide, sketch designs inside the bowl also.

Pinch Pots

The people who live in the Southwest—the Zuni, Hopi, Acoma, Santo Domingo, and Taos—are wonderful potters. They shape clay bowls by hand, and decorate them with stylized designs that are like the work of the ancient people of the region, the Mimbreños.

You can make a simple bowl from clay. The bowls are called pinch pots because you shape them by pinching the clay with your fingers.

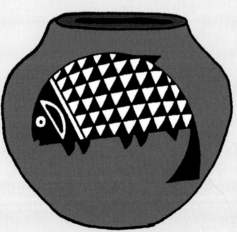
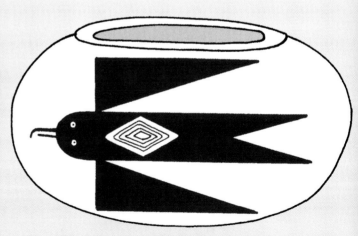

Here's What You Need:
- pinch pots made from clay
- poster or acrylic paints, brushes, newspaper
- clear nail polish

Here's How You Do It:
- Follow the directions on page 14 to make small pinch pots. Bake them (page 47) for five minutes and let them cool.
- Choose a design and study it to see the shapes that make it up. The turtle is the quickest to draw; look at the illustrations to see how to do it step-by-step. Paint on the first shape and then finish the design. (If you use acrylic paint, cover your work surfaces with newspaper.) Paint on other designs.
- When the paint is dry, apply clear nail polish to seal the designs and make them shine.

Mimbreños Drawings of "Wild Brothers"

Very long ago the trees, the animals and birds, and fish, also the grass and rocks, and mountains, and all things in Nature could talk together, including people, who in turn could talk to them. And so all things came to know each other and to understand each other better.

—Hopi Wise Man

The Mimbreños lived about a thousand years ago along the Mimbres River, in what is now New Mexico. These Native Americans made pots from local clay and painted them white. Then, using twigs or long, slender leaves for brushes, and paint made from powdered clays, plants, and minerals, they drew on simple, bold, figures. The designs show the animals of the Mimbreño world—the people's "wild brothers." ◙

• You can also use these designs on posters or on a bulletin board. Paint several designs onto a large piece of fabric to make a mural or wall hanging.

18

19

Here's What You Need:
- pencil, rocks or shells
- colored permanent markers
- gold or silver paint markers

Here's How You Do It:
- Using a pencil, draw designs freehand on some clean rocks or shells.
- Draw over the pencil lines with black and colored markers. For a different effect, go over some details with a gold or silver paint marker.

Shell and Rock Drawings

The ancient people who lived in the American Southwest left records of their lives in petroglyphs, or pictures scratched onto rocks with a stone tool. If you look hard at the petroglyph designs here, you can find buffalo, bears, wolves, coyotes, lizards, serpents, insects, horses, deer, antelope, bighorn sheep, turtles, and people. Other designs show the sun, moon, stars, lightning, clouds, rain, corn, trails, water springs, and the dwelling places of the spirits. You can paint these designs on rocks or shells.

Here's What You Need:
- paper, pencil
- black, gold, or silver markers or permanent fabric markers
- T-shirt, stones, or note cards

Here's How You Do It:
- Trace a design and transfer it (page 46) to paper or a T-shirt, or other material. Use a copying machine to enlarge the design to decorate a shirt. Draw it on note cards, as a messenger of "good spirits." You can draw the design freehand on a stone and use it as a paperweight.
- Go over the pencil lines with a black marker or fabric marker. Try going over some lines with a gold or silver marker.

Kokopelli, the Flute Player

Kokopelli, the flute player, is seen in petroglyphs throughout the Southwest. The drawings here are copied from these carvings on stone. Kokopelli appears in several legends. In one, he is a traveling peddler who plays a flute to let villagers know that he comes in peace. In others, he is the god of the harvest, or the "water sprinkler," who brings rain and floods. Sometimes he is a traveling minstrel, with a sack of songs on his back. Kokopelli's image varies, but he is always shown with a curved back, a long body, and holding a flute.

Here's What You Need:
- homemade clay (page 47)
- pencil, tracing paper, scissors, butter knife
- poster or acrylic paints, brushes, newspaper, clear nail polish
- cardboard, white paper, feathers, beads, fabric scraps
- toothpick, string

Here's How You Do It:
- Pinch off a piece of clay about 4 inches (10 cm) long. Flatten the piece until it is 1/2 inch (1.2 cm) thick.
- Choose a design and draw it on the clay, or trace the shape to make a pattern (page 46), cut it out, and place it on your flattened clay.
- With a knife, cut out the animal from the clay. Gently shape it for more detail and a three-dimensional look. Press in eyes and draw a mouth with a pencil. Bake it (page 47) and let it cool.

Zuni Animal Figures

The Zuni people make small carvings of animals from clay, wood, shells, or stones. Each figure has its own spirit. The carvings are used in ceremonies to bring luck in hunting and fishing; and to ensure health, a long life, healthy children, success in love, and a good harvest.

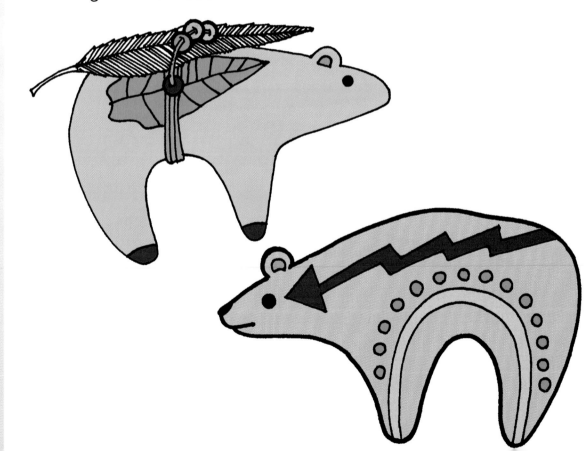

Turquoise, black onyx, sandstone, amber, lapis lazuli and other stones are often used. Contrasting materials are used for the animal's features and for offerings placed on the animal's back as a gift to the spirit. Choose from the designs here to make clay figures of a bear, bird, snake, fox, lizard, rabbit, owl, fish, frog, squirrel, turtle, or horse. ◈

- Paint the figure, let it dry, and apply a coat of clear nail polish.
- Draw a small arrowhead on cardboard. Cut it out and paint it. Add a real feather or one cut out of paper and painted. Add a few beads; either readymade ones or some that you have made. To make beads, roll small balls of clay and poke a hole through each one with a toothpick. Bake and paint them. Put all these items on a fabric scrap, shape it into a bundle, and tie a string around it. Tie the bundle onto the animal's back. This traditional bundle is thought to give the animal power.
- To make a Zuni necklace, shape several small figures. Poke a hole through each one with a toothpick. Bake them, let them cool, and paint them. Pull a string through the holes, adding some small beads between the figures.

Apache Face Paint

In early days, the Apache were a nomadic people who hunted and gathered wild plants. Later, they began to grow corn and squash. Women played an important role in family life and could own land and become medicine women. The Apache rode horses well and were wonderful hunters. They sometimes decorated their faces and bodies for ceremonies and for battles. We will make colorful paint that is safe to use to decorate your face and hands.

Here's What You Need:
- paper cups or small bowls
- measuring spoons and mixing spoons
- cold cream
- cornstarch
- water
- food coloring

Here's How You Do It:
- Use a different bowl or paper cup for each color you want to make. Red and blue are especially good colors to try.
- Mix one tablespoon of cold cream, two tablespoons of cornstarch, and one table-spoon of water in a bowl or cup. Add a few drops of food coloring and stir.
- Repeat for each additional color you want to make.
- Paint Apache designs on your face and hands, using your fingers or cotton swabs. Keep the paint away from your eyes.

Here's What You Need:
- 21 twigs
- string, black marker

Here's How You Do It:
- Collect your twigs. Choose 12 twigs for the body. Hold them in a bundle and wrap the string around them. Tie a knot to secure the bundle.
- Select a thick twig for the neck and tie it onto the body. Pick a short, thick twig for the head and tie it onto the neck. With a black marker, draw on two eyes.
- Choose two twigs with several short branches for antlers. Tie them onto the head.
- Choose four medium-width twigs that seem the right length for legs. Look for twigs with a little branch at the bottom, to give the appearance of a hoof. Tie the legs to the body.
- Insert a small thick twig into the body for a tail.

Ancient Split Twig Deer

Now comes the deer up to our house.
He brings the needed food of life,
While we give needed food to him.

—Song of the Tewa

This Southwestern twig deer has been made for hundreds of years from willow reeds and flexible twigs. The people valued the deer; it provided meat and skins for clothing and other items. The twig deer is an offering to bring a good hunt and good fortune for the tribe.

Native American Moccasins

Native Americans believe moccasins should be beautiful, because the foot should be as lovely as the grasses and flowers that are walked upon. Traditional moccasins are made of animal hides. Ours are made from a pair of heavyweight socks, such as athletic socks.

Here's What You Need:
- heavyweight socks: tan, gray, brown, or dark green
- pencil, ruler, scissors, glue
- light cardboard, oaktag, or light-colored felt
- colored felt or fabric markers

Here's How You Do It:
- Flatten the socks. With scissors, cut off the tops, starting 3 inches (7.5 cm) above the heel and slanting up to the front. These will be the basic moccasins.
- To make decorative panels, cut out two 3 inch (7.5 cm) by 4 inch (10 cm) pieces of cardboard, oaktag, or felt. Choose designs: patterns, flowers, or symbols—horse tracks, bird, mountain, lightning, the four directions, or others. Cut out pieces of felt to make the figures. Glue them onto the panels. If you prefer, draw them on with markers.
- Glue the design panels onto the socks.

Here's What You Need:
- homemade clay (page 47)
- poster paints, brushes
- cardboard, glue, twigs

Here's How You Do It:
- Flatten the clay with your hands. Shape one house. Add another house onto it so that the houses share the wall between them. Add more buildings, as you like.
- Bake the village (page 47). After it has cooled, paint it in an earth color. Outline the windows with blue.
- Glue the village onto a piece of cardboard. Make a few small ladders by gluing twigs together. Lean the ladders against the walls of some houses.

A Pueblo Village

Pueblo is a Spanish word that has several meanings—a village, a culture, a type of Native American architecture. In the 1500s, Spanish explorers gave this name to the people they found living along the Rio Grande River.

In the Southwest today, some pueblo dwellings are ancient ruins, but others are still lived in. Pueblo villages are groups of box-like buildings made of stone or of clay and mud bricks (adobe). Neighboring houses are often joined together. The houses have a number of stories, with terraces and flat roofs. Ladders lead to the upper levels. The thick walls are plastered over with a clay mixture to look smooth. The inside of the house is white; the outside is an earth color to blend into the landscape. Window frames are painted sky blue to bring good spirits. We will make a miniature pueblo village.

Here's What You Need:
- pencil, scissors, glue
- scraps of white and colored felt or other cloth
- large piece of white felt, cotton, or other cloth
- tissues, rubber bands, twigs, yarn or string
- fine-line marker, paints, brushes
- 10 inch (25 cm) by 16 inch (40 cm) piece of printed cloth
- stapler, beads, feathers

Here's How You Do It:
- To decorate a shawl or blanket, cut out the pieces to make up the design from colored felt, following the illustration. Glue the pieces onto white felt or heavy cloth. A full-sized blanket could be a shawl for you or a friend. A small version could be a shawl for a scrap doll.

Navajo Designs for a Blanket and a Scrap Doll

Navajo land spreads from Arizona, to New Mexico, and into Utah. The Navajo people have lived here for over 500 years. They make beautiful pottery and jewelry, and woolen blankets, rugs, and clothing woven on hand looms. Three traditional Navajo blanket designs are shown (pages 34–35): a Chief's Blanket with stripes and diamonds, a design called Eye Dazzler, and the Tree of Life. Navajo women use the blankets as shawls. You can draw these designs freehand or trace them and enlarge them using a copying machine. Draw them on cotton fabric to make wall hangings or floor cloths. Paint them on T-shirts. Or make a large card with a design on the outside, and write a Navajo poem from pages 44–45 inside.

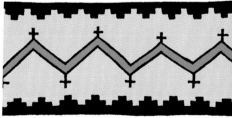

- To make a doll, shape several tissues into a ball for the head. Cover this ball with a scrap of fabric. Put a rubber band around the bottom to hold it. Insert a stick or twig into the head for a neck and body, and secure with glue.
- Draw a face with a marker. Make braids from yarn or string and glue them on.
- Use printed cloth for a skirt, or paint plain cloth in sky colors. Take the long edge of the cloth and fold it into pleats to make a waist. Staple the pleats closed. Glue the cloth to the stick body.
- Drape the blanket over the doll's shoulders. Overlap the front edges and glue them together. Add a string of beads and place a feather in the doll's hair.

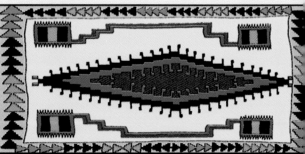

33

TREE OF LIFE

EYE DAZZLER

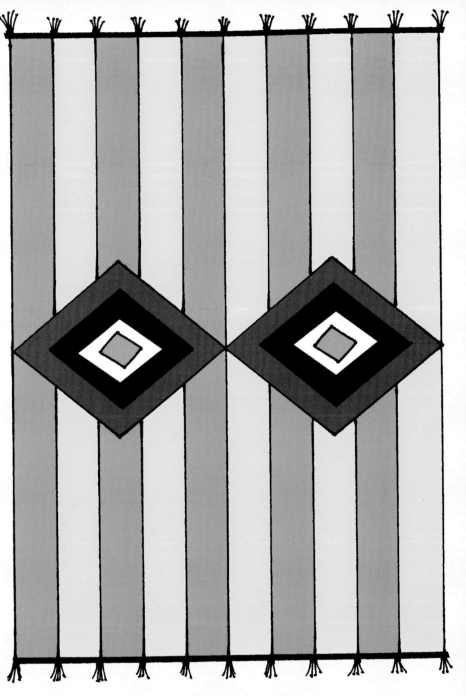

CHIEF'S BLANKET

Here's What You Need:
- tracing paper, pencil
- sandpaper sheets
- black permanent fine-line marker
- poster paints, brushes

Here's How You Do It:
- Trace and transfer (page 46) the designs onto the sandpaper. Or draw the designs freehand. Go over the lines with a black marker.
- Use poster paints to color in the designs.

Sky Mother and Sky Father Sand Paintings

Navajo sand painting is an old art form. Dry paintings are made by letting powdered, colored rock and earth flow between the fingers onto a flat bed of sand on the ground. The paintings are made under the watchful eye of a medicine person, and they are destroyed before sundown on the day they are made. These paintings are traditionally thought to have healing powers. The person for whom the painting is made comes away with a peaceful mind and a sense of harmony with the world. Here are two designs for paintings on sandpaper: Sky Mother and Sky Father. These figures are intended to bring rain. ◈

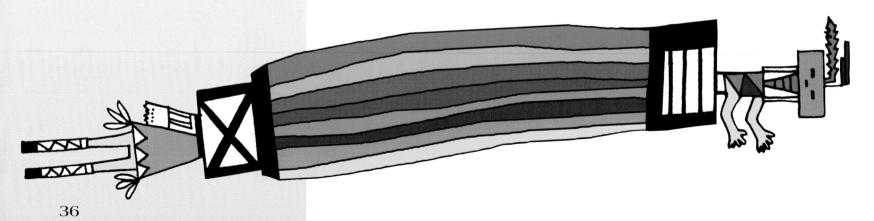

Here's What You Need:
- homemade clay (page 47), pencil
- poster or acrylic paint, brushes, newspaper
- fine-line permanent markers, glue

Here's How You Do It:
- Pull off a handful of clay and shape the storyteller figure. With a pencil, make an open mouth.
- Pull off smaller amounts of clay to make the listening figures.
- Bake the figures for 10 to 15 minutes (page 47). Remove them from the oven when they are lightly browned.

Pueblo Storytellers

Since ancient times, Pueblo potters have made clay storytelling figures. The classic figure is a grandmother who passes down stories and traditions to her grandchildren. Today other storytelling figures are also made, such as grandfathers, owls, or bears. They all have open mouths and are surrounded by listening children. We will make a clay storyteller.

- When the figures are cool, paint them. If you use acrylic paint, protect your work surfaces with newspaper.
- Use fine-line markers to draw on noses, eyes, and designs on the clothing. Glue the small figures to the story-teller if you like.

Here's What You Need:
- homemade clay (page 47)
- pencil, butter knife
- tracing paper, drawing paper, scissors, fine-line black permanent marker, string
- acrylic paints, brushes, newspaper
- white glue, clear nail polish
- copper wire, black beads, scraps of felt, safety pins

Here's How You Do It:
- For a pendant, flatten a handful of clay to 1/2 inch (1.2 cm) thickness. Trace and transfer (page 46) the pendant design onto paper. Cut it out. Place this pattern on the clay and draw around it. With a knife, cut out the pendant shape.
- Poke a hole near the top of the pendant. Make it large enough for a string to pass through. Bake the pendant for 5 minutes (page 47).

Southwestern Jewelry

Native Americans of the Southwest make handsome jewelry using local materials. Silver and turquoise jewelry is especially prized. We will make a pendant with a Hopi bear claw design or a Navajo dancer design, and Zuni creature pins.

HOPI BEAR CLAW

NAVAJO DANCER

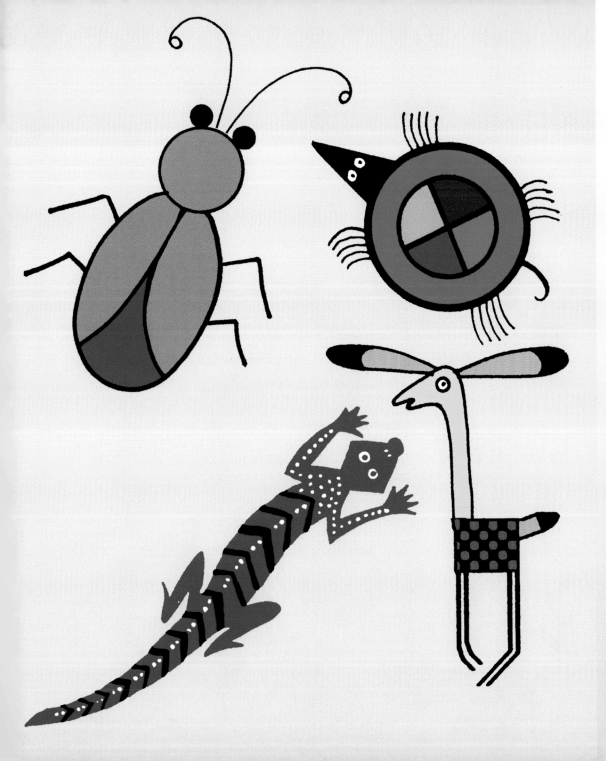

- With a black marker, draw on the details of the design. Paint it in. (Cover your work surface with newspaper.)
- Coat the pendant with clear nail polish. When dry, pull a string through the hole. Make a knot above the pendant. Knot the ends of the string together so you can wear the pendant.
- For a creature pin, shape the body and head from clay. Make the back of the body flat and the front rounded. For the lizard, also shape legs. For the whirly bird, shape ears and a tail.
- Bake the pieces for 5 minutes. Let them cool, then glue the head and other parts to the body.
- With scissors, cut pieces of wire. Shape wire legs and antennae for the beetle, legs and a tail for the turtle, and legs for the whirly bird. Glue them on.
- Paint the creature. When dry, add a coat of clear nail polish. Let it dry, then glue it onto a felt scrap. Glue a safety pin to the back of the felt.

41

Here's What You Need:

Ingredients
- 2 cups all-purpose flour
- 2 cups cornmeal
- 3 tablespoons baking powder
- 1 teaspoon baking soda
- 1 teaspoon salt
- 2 cups milk
- 1 tablespoon vegetable oil
- extra oil for frying the bread
- extra flour to sprinkle on working surface

Utensils
- large mixing bowl, mixing spoon
- measuring cups and spoons
- aluminum foil, plate
- knife, long-handled fork
- frying pan
- paper towels

Here's How You Do It:
- Ask an adult to help when you fry the bread. Before you start, wash your hands.
- In a mixing bowl, combine the flour, cornmeal, baking powder, baking soda, and salt.

Native American Bread

The Earth is my Mother,
She takes care of me.
The Earth is my Mother,
I take care of her.

—Native American Chant

In ancient times, Native Americans depended upon nature's bounty for their food. In time, the people learned to plant seeds and grow crops. The main crop was maize, or corn, that was ground into a fine powder or flour and used to make bread and other foods. Pueblo women bake cornbread in outdoor ovens called hornos. This recipe is for Native American style bread.

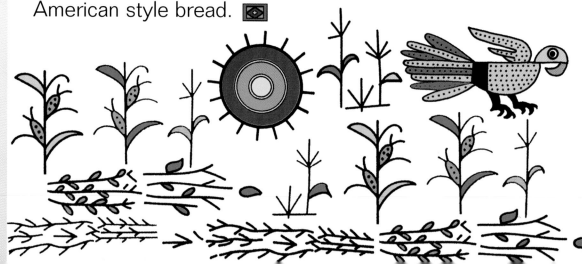

- Make a hole in the center of the mixture and pour in the milk and vegetable oil. Stir until combined.
- Sprinkle some flour on a work surface and place the dough on it. Knead the dough gently, form it into a ball, and let it rest for fifteen minutes.
- Cut the dough into eight pieces. Flatten the pieces with your hands until they are the size of saucers, about 6 inches (15 cm) across. Stack them on a plate between sheets of aluminum foil.
- With an adult helping, heat the oil in a frying pan. Place one flat round of dough in the pan. The dough will quickly puff up and turn brown. Using a long-handled fork, turn the bread over to brown the other side. Remove the bread from the pan and place it on a paper towel to drain.
- Repeat this process for all eight pieces of bread.

Here's What You Need:
- paper and pencil or pen
- colored pencils, markers

Here's How You Do It:
- Choose a poem and write it out on a piece of white paper.
- Make a border with designs from this book. Use different colored pencils and markers.

Native American Writings

These poems and songs have been adapted from traditional writings of Native Americans of California, the Great Basin, and the Southwest. You can write one out and add designs to make a wall piece or poster, or put some in a handmade book.

Sun

The Star Story
When the world was being made,
When the Gods were placing stars in patterns in the sky,
Coyote stole the star bag.
Coyote spilled the stars out in the sky,
Helter skelter in the sky,
When the world was being made.

—Navajo

What is a Man?
A man is nothing
*   without his family.*
He is of less importance
*   than the bug*
*   crossing the trail.*

—Pomo

Sunflower

I see the Earth.
I am looking at Her and smile
    because She makes me happy.
The Earth, looking back at me,
    is smiling too.
May I walk happily
    and lightly
    upon Her.

—Navajo

corn

Song of the Young War God
I have been to the end of the earth.
I have been to the end of the waters.
I have been to the end of the sky.
I have been to the end of the mountains.
I have found that none were my friends.

—Navajo

Come and sing!
Come and sing in the old way,
Come and make the sun shine
So the corn will grow,
The squash will grow,
The beans will grow.

—Hopi

Plants are thought to be alive,
    their juice is their blood,
    and they grow.
The same is true of trees.
All things die.
Therefore all things have life.
Because all things have life,
    gifts have to be given to
    all things.

—Pomo

It was the wind
    that gave them life.
It is the wind
    that comes out of our mouths
    that gives us life.
When this ceases to blow we die.
In the skin at the tips of our fingers
    we see the trail of the wind;
    it shows us the wind blew
    when our ancestors were created.

—Navajo

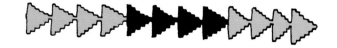

Basic Techniques

Tracing Designs

Here's What You Need:

- tracing paper
- pencil, tape
- drawing paper, fabric, or other material

Here's How You Do It:

- Place tracing paper over the design you want to trace. If you like, tape the paper down. Trace the lines of the design, pressing firmly on your pencil.
- Remove the tape and turn the paper over. On the back, draw over the lines of the design with the side of your pencil point.
- Turn the tracing paper right side up and place it on a sheet of drawing paper or the material for your project. You may tape this down. Draw over the lines. This will transfer the design onto the paper or the material. ◈

Making Clay

Here's What You Need:

- 2 cups flour plus extra flour to sprinkle on the work surface
- 1 cup salt
- 1 cup water
- large bowl, spoon, measuring cup
- cookie sheet, potholders, aluminum foil

Here's How You Do It:

- Use this recipe to make clay for projects in this book. Additional instructions are given with the specific projects.
- Mix the flour and salt in a bowl. Add the water a little at a time. Mix the clay well with your hands until it is smooth. The clay is ready to roll out and cut, or to shape according to the project directions.
- If you need to bake the clay, ask an adult to help you use the oven. Heat the oven to 325° F. (165° C.). Line a cookie sheet with aluminum foil and place the clay pieces on it, spacing them 1 inch (2.5 cm) apart. Bake until lightly browned, 15 to 20 minutes, but check often to see that the edges are not burning.
- Using potholders, remove the cookie sheet from the oven. Allow the clay to cool. Paint or decorate it following the project instructions. ◈

Index